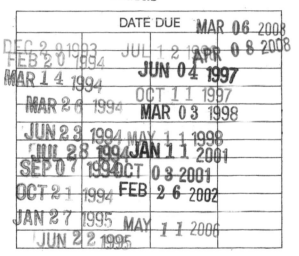

SHARKS

Design	David West
	Children's Book Design
Designer	Keith Newell
Editor	Charles DeVere
Picture Researcher	Emma Krikler
Illustrator	Darren Evans

© Aladdin Books 1992

First published in
the United States in 1992 by
Gloucester Press
95 Madison Avenue
New York, NY 10016

Library of Congress Cataloging-in-Publication Data

Robson, Denny.
    Sharks / by Denny Robson.
        p.   cm. -- (Let's look up)
    Includes index.
    Summary: Discusses the different species of sharks, creatures
found in every ocean.
    ISBN 0-531-17354-2
    1. Sharks--Juvenile literature. (1. Sharks.) I. Title.
QL638.9.R63   1992
597'.31--dc20   91-34966   CIP   AC

Printed in Belgium

LET'S LOOK UP

SHARKS

DENNY ROBSON

FRANKLIN WATTS
New York: London: Toronto: Sydney

Contents

About this book

You can decide for yourself
how to read this book. You
can simply read it straight
through, or you can follow
the arrows to find out more
about a subject before you
go on. The choice is yours!

Follow the arrows if you want to know more....

Introduction

Many people think of sharks as savage monsters with terrible teeth, ready to attack any swimmer who passes by. A few large sharks do attack humans, but most are harmless – unless you're a fish! Sharks first began swimming in the world's oceans 400 million years ago, even before the dinosaurs appeared. There are now over 350 different species, in all sorts of strange and wonderful shapes and sizes.

△ The terrifying great white – star of the horror film "Jaws"

A swimming machine

A shark's body is streamlined, which means it is shaped for moving quickly and easily through the water. Its fins keep it balanced and help it to steer, while its strong tail drives it along great distances at steady speeds. The shark can travel at 20 mph to catch its prey, diving and turning sharply without effort. It is a perfect swimming machine.

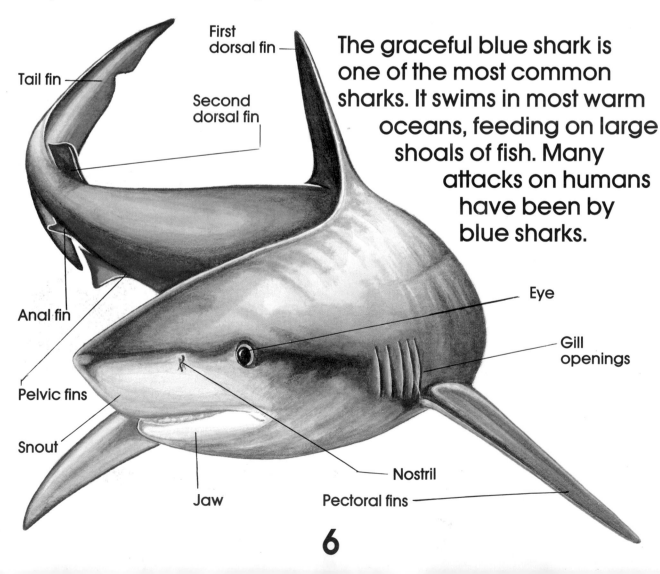

The graceful blue shark is one of the most common sharks. It swims in most warm oceans, feeding on large shoals of fish. Many attacks on humans have been by blue sharks.

First dorsal fin

Tail fin

Second dorsal fin

Anal fin

Pelvic fins

Snout

Jaw

Nostril

Eye

Gill openings

Pectoral fins

How big are sharks?

The blue shark can grow to 15ft. But sharks come in a wide variety of sizes, from the tiny dwarf shark (6 inches) to the enormous whale shark (50 feet).

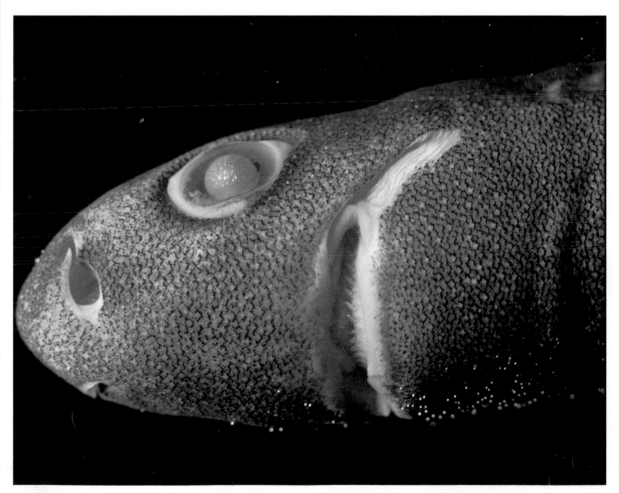

△ This strange creature is a dwarf shark.

Find out more about shark sizes in Sharks worldwide PAGE 26

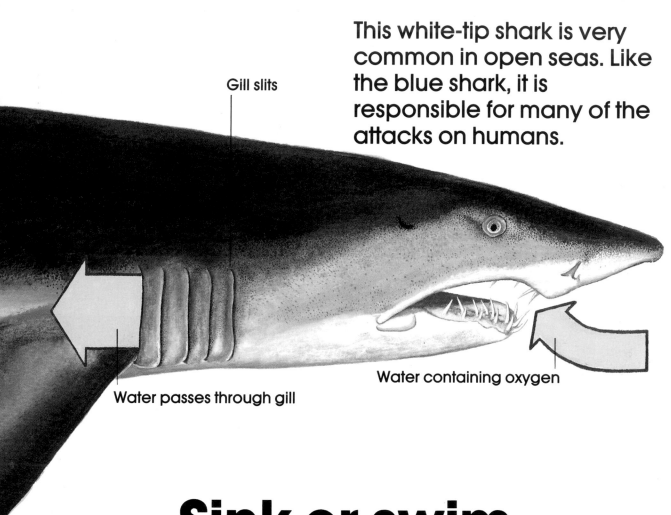

This white-tip shark is very common in open seas. Like the blue shark, it is responsible for many of the attacks on humans.

Gill slits

Water passes through gill

Water containing oxygen

Sink or swim

Sharks do not have an air sac to keep them afloat, like other fish. Continuous movement and their oily liver helps them to float. Sharks that live near the surface of the sea, like the blue or the white-tip, keep swimming all their lives. As they swim, they take in oxygen from the water through slits called gills. If they stopped moving, they would drown!

Do sharks ever sleep?

Surface-swimming sharks do not stop and sleep. But sharks that live on the seabed, like this angel shark, may lie still for hours. We still do not know very much about how sharks live, although scientists are trying to find out more about them.

Find out more about shark science in Sharkwatching facts → PAGE 30

King of fish

Sharks have no air sac, like other fish, and there are other differences, too. They do not have bones, as fish do. Their skeleton is made of a gristly material called cartilage. Their skin is also different. Fish have scales, but sharks have rough leathery skins, covered in sharp points. Swimmers have been badly hurt just by brushing against a shark's thorny skin.

The tough skin of a shark is dotted with sharp points which are sometimes called "skinteeth." They are very like our own teeth.

Why are sharks dark on top and paler underneath?

Most sharks are colored this way so that they cannot be seen from above or below. Sharks that live on the seabed, like the wobbegong, are camouflaged to blend in with their background.

△ The mako shark, showing the difference between its back and belly

Find out more about the wobbegong in Unusual sharkfacts PAGE 28

Jaws of a Tiger Shark

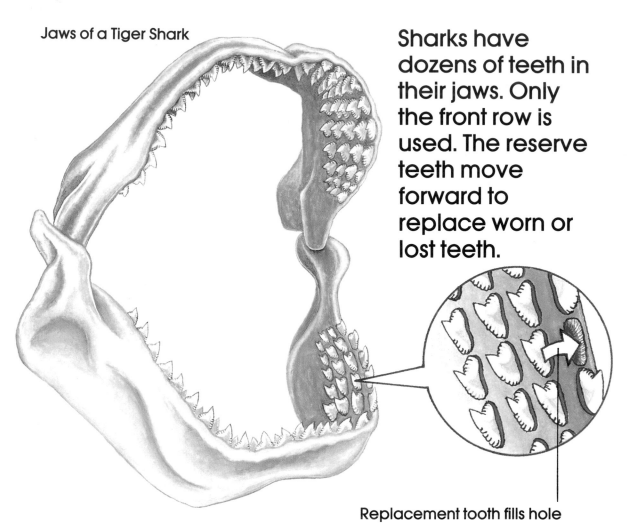

Sharks have dozens of teeth in their jaws. Only the front row is used. The reserve teeth move forward to replace worn or lost teeth.

Replacement tooth fills hole

Teeth and jaws

Sharks can bite with enormous power. Their jaws can be three hundred times stronger than a human's jaw. They have rows and rows of teeth, which can be as hard as steel. As front teeth wear out, they are replaced by new teeth from inside the jaw. So the shark's teeth are always razor sharp. A shark may have thousands of teeth in its lifetime.

△ A shark seizes prey in its strong jaws.

Do all sharks have the same kind of teeth?

The shape of a shark's teeth depends on the food it eats. The Port Jackson has flat teeth for crushing shellfish. The great white has shearing teeth to tear chunks of dolphin or sea lion. Giant sharks have tiny teeth.

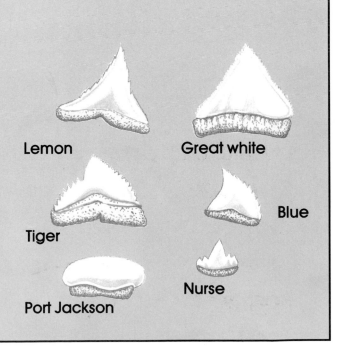

Lemon

Great white

Tiger

Blue

Port Jackson

Nurse

Find out more about giant sharks in Unusual sharkfacts PAGE 28

shark senses

A shark relies more on its sense of smell than on its sight, to track down prey. It can smell a drop of blood, even when it is diluted ten million times, and go racing in for the kill. Some sharks have special cells on their snouts which pick up tiny electrical signals from their prey. Sensitive areas of their skin pick up vibrations made by creatures struggling in the sea nearby.

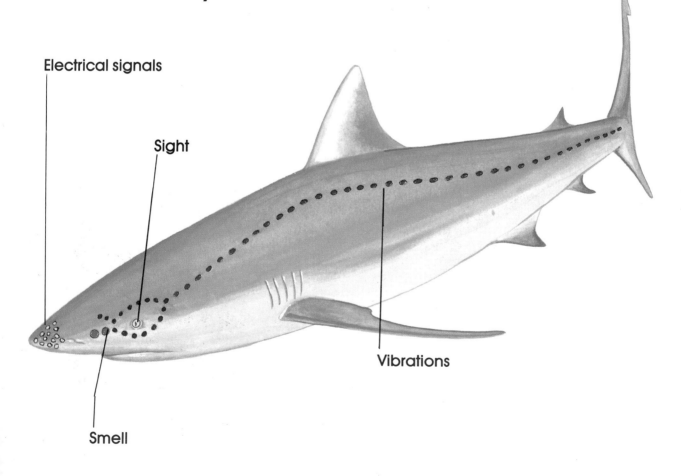

Electrical signals

Sight

Vibrations

Smell

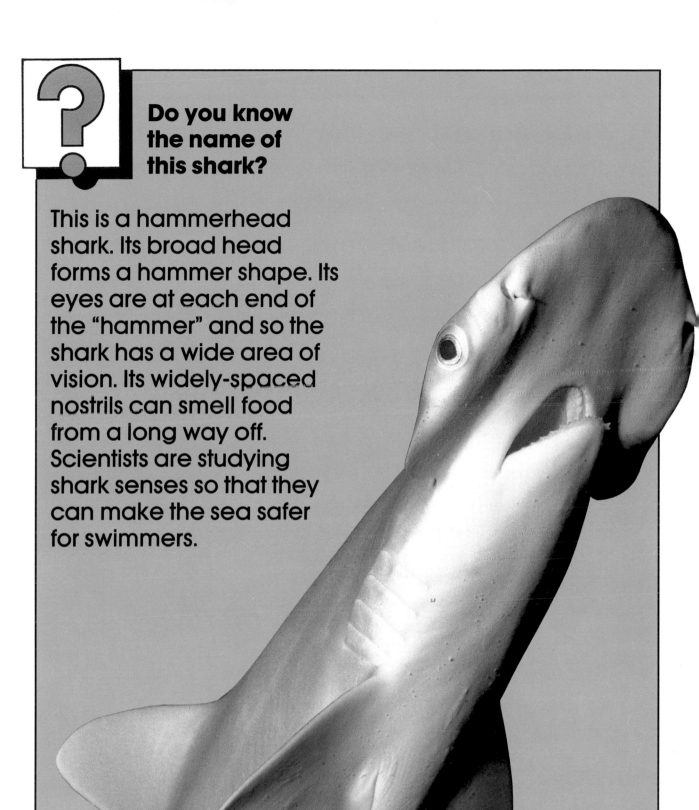

This is a hammerhead shark. Its broad head forms a hammer shape. Its eyes are at each end of the "hammer" and so the shark has a wide area of vision. Its widely-spaced nostrils can smell food from a long way off. Scientists are studying shark senses so that they can make the sea safer for swimmers.

If you want to know how scientists study sharks, turn to **Sharkwatching facts**

PAGE 30

15

Feeding

Sharks spend most of their lives looking for things to eat. Most eat fish, but some will eat anything that comes their way! The tiger shark will munch old boots and paint cans, as well as turtles and sea birds. People think of the great white as a man-eater, but it would prefer to eat seals, dolphins, or even whales. It can cram 100lb into its stomach in one meal.

This is what a tiger shark might eat. Not surprisingly, it has been called the garbage can of the sea!

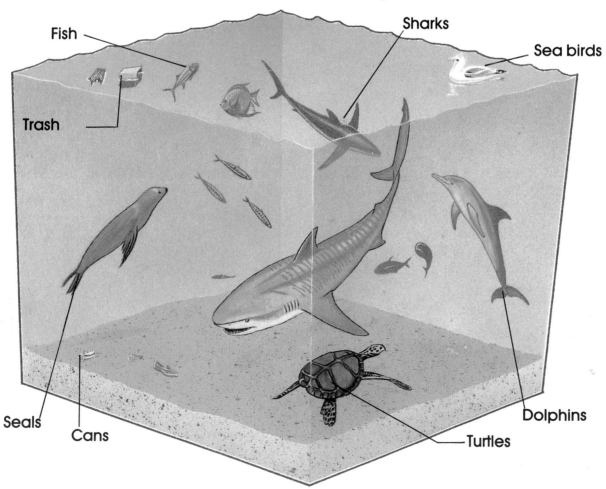

Fish

Sharks

Sea birds

Trash

Seals

Cans

Turtles

Dolphins

What is a "feeding frenzy?"

Sometimes, several sharks go for the same prey and the sharks go crazy. They twist and turn wildly, biting anything that moves, including each other!

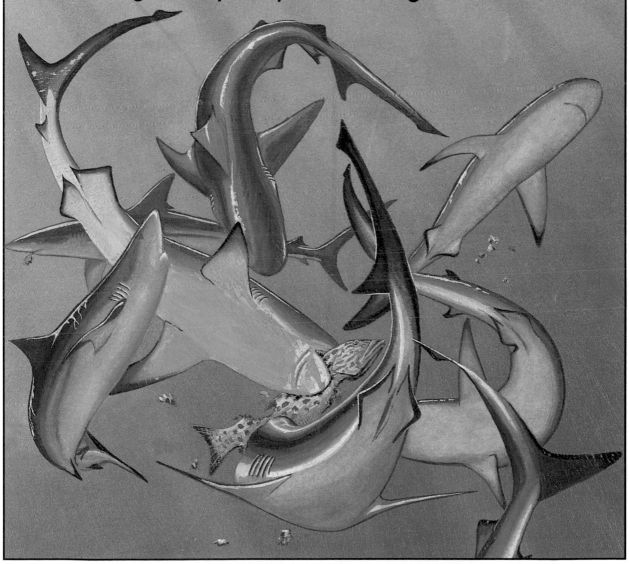

If you want to know more about sharks attacking each other, turn to Shark enemies

PAGE 22

Shark babies

The whale shark and the dogfish lay eggs, just like other fish. But the eggs have tough leathery cases to protect the young sharks until they are ready to hatch themselves. Many other sharks give birth to live babies. The young pups can take care of themselves and hunt right away. While the young of the sand tiger shark are still inside their mother, they eat each other until only two are left!

The dogfish, a small shark, lays eggs in tough little cases which are sometimes called mermaids' purses. It takes several months for the young to hatch. You can sometimes find the empty cases washed up on beaches.

How many pups do sharks have?

Different sharks have different numbers of young. The blue shark may have 50 pups at one time. The porbeagle develops many eggs inside her. But as the first hatch, they eat the yolk of the other eggs, so that only one or two pups are born.

▽ A young tiger shark

If you want to know more about the range of different sharks, turn to Sharks worldwide

PAGE 26

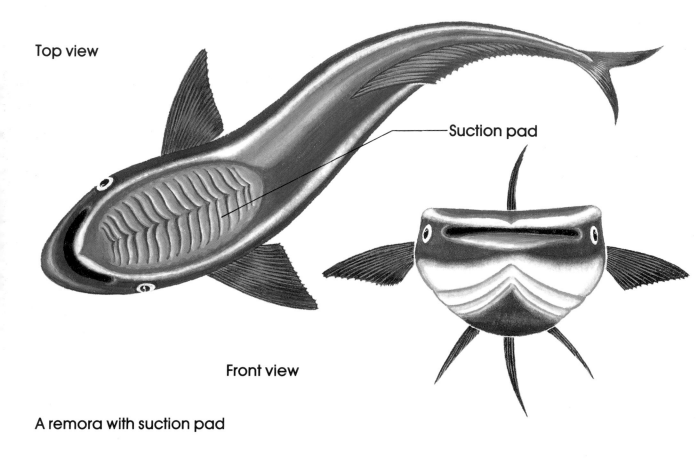

Top view

Suction pad

Front view

A remora with suction pad

Partners

Striped pilot fish often swim alongside sharks. They act as cleaners of the shark's skin and also feed on scraps of food left over from a kill. Other strange fish called remoras actually cling on to the shark. They use large suckers on their heads to hitch a ride. When they jump off to feed on the shark's leftovers, they are lucky that their host leaves them alone!

Do sharks swim with other sharks?

Most sharks hunt alone, like this white-tip, below. But some sharks may travel in large schools, like the basking shark. The thresher shark hunts in packs, rounding up fish with its long tail.

△ A leopard shark with remoras.

If you want to know more about the thresher shark, turn to Unusual sharkfacts

PAGE 28

Killer and sperm whales attack sharks. Dolphins attack in groups to protect their young.

Shark enemies

Many sharks are large and fierce and few animals attack them. But smaller sharks are preyed on by a number of enemies, including other sharks. When a shark is about to give birth, she has to swim to different waters in case her own kind eat the young. If the mother herself meets a pup later, *she* may eat it! But the shark's biggest enemies are humans.

Why do people attack sharks?

People kill about 4.5 million sharks each year. Some are killed to protect beaches, others simply for sport, and many are killed for food. Some are caught so that they can be studied by scientists.

△ Fishermen catching a hammerhead shark

If you want to know more about sharks in captivity, turn to Sharkwatching facts

PAGE 30

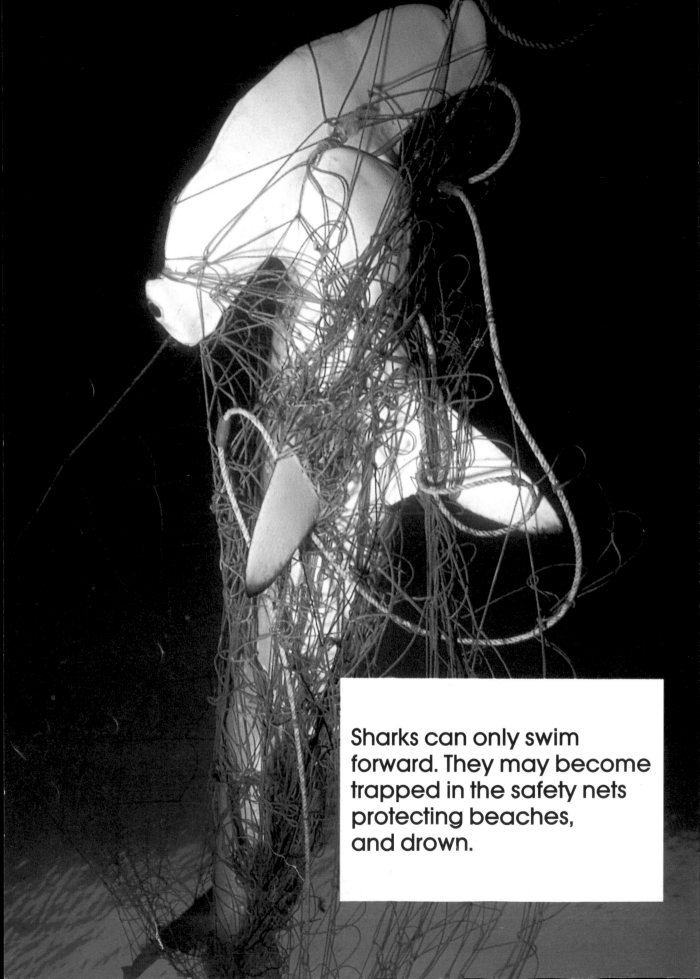

Sharks can only swim forward. They may become trapped in the safety nets protecting beaches, and drown.

Shark attack!

No one knows how many people have been killed by sharks. There are perhaps 100 attacks on people each year, but most victims survive. The warm waters around the coasts of Australia, South Africa, and the warmer coasts of North America are the most dangerous. Swimmers in these areas must take care and obey the safety rules.

Which shark is most dangerous to humans?

The great white

Only about 30 of the 350 species of shark have been known to attack humans. The most feared is probably the great white shark. Next would be the tiger shark and the bull sharks.

Find out more about where different species of shark live in Sharks worldwide

PAGE 26

Sharks worldwide

This chart shows you some of the more common sharks. They are drawn to scale. The side of each square represents one foot.

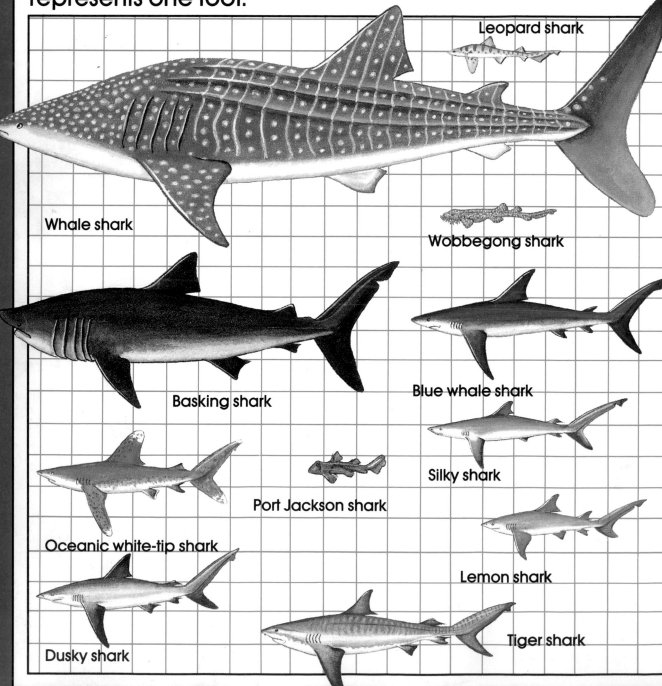

Leopard shark

Whale shark

Wobbegong shark

Basking shark

Blue whale shark

Silky shark

Oceanic white-tip shark

Port Jackson shark

Lemon shark

Dusky shark

Tiger shark

Sharks live throughout the sea, some on the seabed in coastal waters, others in deep trenches and others near the surface.

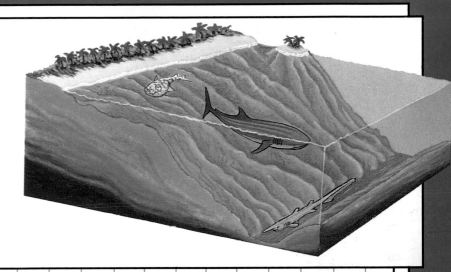

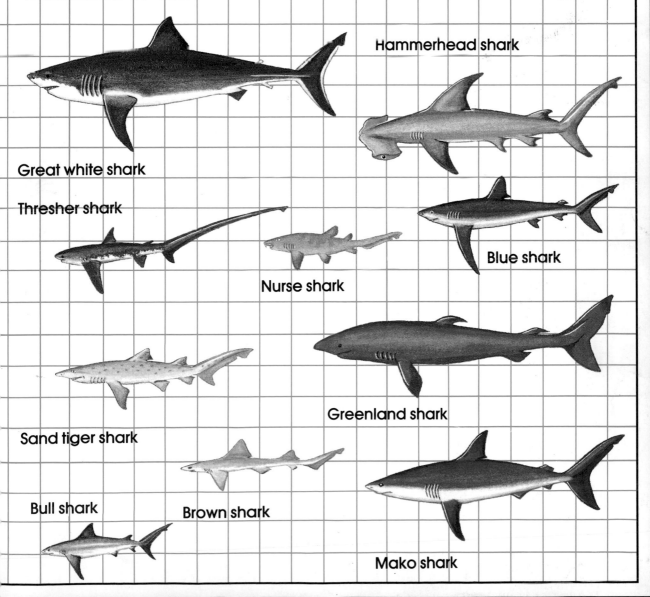

Hammerhead shark

Great white shark

Thresher shark

Nurse shark

Blue shark

Sand tiger shark

Greenland shark

Bull shark

Brown shark

Mako shark

Unusual sharkfacts

Whale shark (50ft)
The whale shark is the biggest fish in the sea and it is harmless. It swims slowly through the water with its huge mouth open to gather the plankton it feeds on.

Basking shark (46ft)
Basking sharks are also gentle giants which feed on plankton, filtering it from the seawater.

Goblin shark (10ft)
This odd-looking shark is perhaps most mysterious of all. It lives in deep oceans.

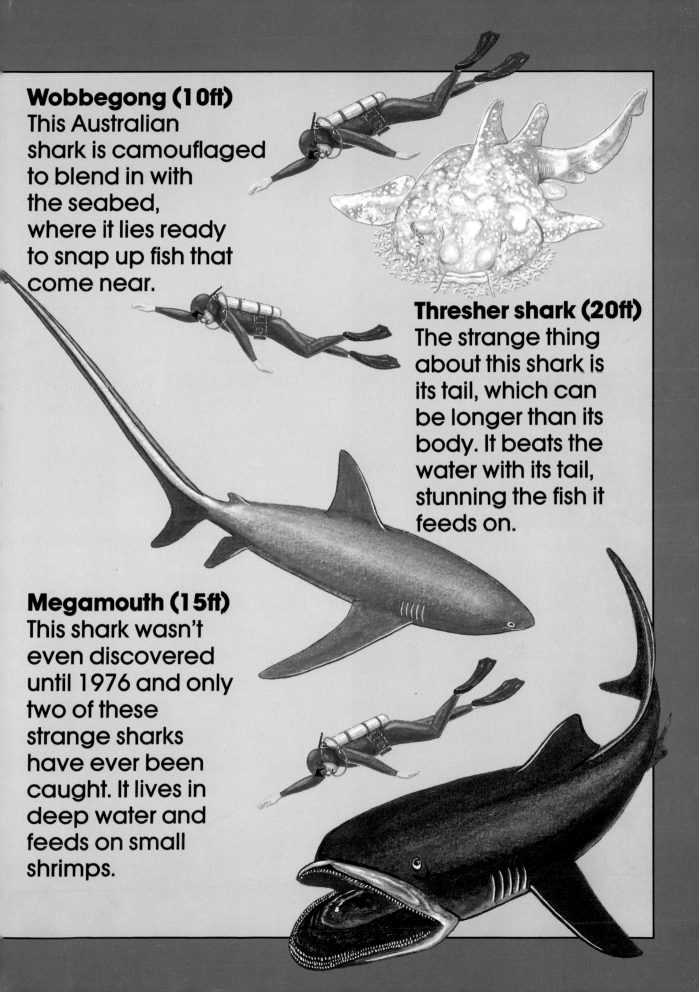

Wobbegong (10ft)
This Australian shark is camouflaged to blend in with the seabed, where it lies ready to snap up fish that come near.

Thresher shark (20ft)
The strange thing about this shark is its tail, which can be longer than its body. It beats the water with its tail, stunning the fish it feeds on.

Megamouth (15ft)
This shark wasn't even discovered until 1976 and only two of these strange sharks have ever been caught. It lives in deep water and feeds on small shrimps.

Sharkwatching fact

Sharks are difficult to study and we still know very little about how they live. But scientists are working to find out more about them. Divers can observe their behavior at sea, and sharks are also studied in captivity.

Sharks kept in pens can be studied to find out more about their learning abilities and their sense of smell and taste. If scientists can discover something sharks dislike, swimmers can carry it with them for protection.

Scientists sometimes swim with sharks to try to understand their movements.

The best place to watch a shark's natural behavior is in the sea. Divers may stay inside a cage for protection. There they can film the sharks in safety.

This scientist is testing her "chain mail" suit. It will protect her from the bites of small sharks.

Glossary

Air sac A sac filled with air that stops a fish from sinking when it is not swimming.

Gills Slits behind the head of fish, used in breathing.

Plankton Tiny floating plants and animals that live in the sea.

Predator An animal that hunts and eats other animals.

Prey An animal hunted by a predator as food.

School A large number of the same kind of fish, all swimming together.

Species Animals and plants that have the same structure and can reproduce together.

Streamlined Shaped to move quickly and easily through water or air.

Index

PHOTOCREDITS
Pages 5 and 31 top: Bruce Coleman Limited; pages 7 and 24: Oxford Scientific Films; pages 9, 11 top and bottom, 13, 15, 19, 21 top and bottom, 30 and 31 bottom: Planet Earth Pictures; page 23, Gamma.